CULTURES OF THE WORLD

ANGOLA

Sean Sheehan

MARSHALL CAVENDISH
New York • London • Sydney

Reference edition published 1999 by
Marshall Cavendish Corporation
99 White Plains Road
Tarrytown
New York 10591

© Times Editions Pte Ltd 1999

Originated and designed by
Times Books International, an imprint of
Times Editions Pte Ltd

Printed in Malaysia

Library of Congress Cataloging-in-Publication Data:

Sheehan, Sean, 1951–
    Angola / Sean Sheehan.
        p. cm.—(Cultures of the World)
    Includes bibliographical references and index.
    Summary: Describes the geography, history, government,
economy, religion, language, arts, leisure, food, festivals, and
lifestyle of this country in west-central Africa.
    ISBN 0-7614-0953-X (lib. bdg.)
    1. Angola—Juvenile literature. [1. Angola.] I. Title.
II. Series.
DT1269.S54   1999
967.3—dc21   98–51963
                    CIP
                    AC

INTRODUCTION

AFTER MORE THAN TWO DECADES OF BLOODY civil war, the young African state of Angola is now in the hopeful process of rebuilding. It is one of the poorest countries on the continent, but with rich natural resources such as oil and diamonds, it has the means and potential to become a prosperous modern state.

Angola's poverty today is not just the result of civil war in recent years but also, like many other parts of Africa, centuries of ruthless exploitation by European colonialists. But now, with colonialism behind it and the end of a crippling civil war in sight, Angolans can look forward to developing their own national identity. This book, part of the *Cultures of the World* series, celebrates Angola's diverse culture and the vibrancy of its people, festivals, music, and lifestyle.

CONTENTS

A girl in Luanda.

CONTENTS

An Angolan mask.

GEOGRAPHY

ANGOLA IS SITUATED IN WEST-CENTRAL AFRICA and is roughly square in shape, with a total area of 481,354 square miles (1,246,700 square km). Extending 793 miles (1,277 km) from north to south and 768 miles (1,236 km) from east to west, it is the second largest country in sub-Saharan Africa. Angola is bordered by the Democratic Republic of Congo (formerly Zaire) to the north and east, Namibia to the south, and Zambia to the east. To the west lies the Atlantic Ocean.

A small part of the country—the province of Cabinda—is physically separated from the rest of Angola by the Congo River. The Cabinda enclave is a short distance north of the outlet of the Congo River, which forms part of Angola's northern border with the Democratic Republic of Congo. The province of Cabinda is surrounded by the Democratic Republic of Congo and Congo.

Opposite: **The imposing Tundavala Gorge.**

Left: **The Atlantic coast near the Luanda oil refinery.**

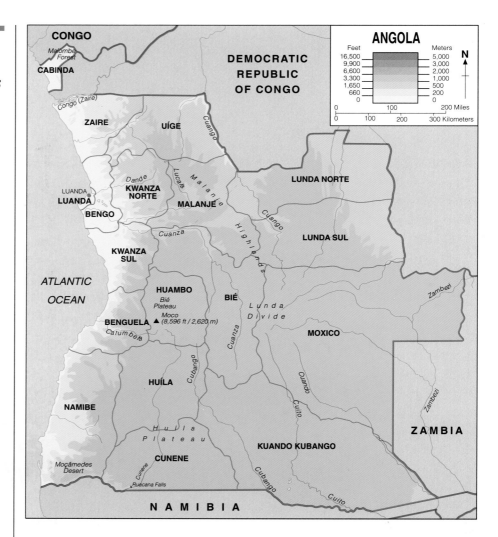

THE SHAPE OF THE LAND

Most of the country lies on a large plateau which, on average, is about 3,950 feet (1,200 m) above sea level. Some parts of the plateau rise to more than 6,500 feet (2,000 m) above sea level, with the highest points being Mount Moco, at 8,596 feet (2,620 m), and Mount Meco, just 121 feet (37 m) lower. Over time erosion by water and wind has shaped the plateau. Geographers call it the "Great Escarpment" (an escarpment is a steep slope or cliff) to describe the effects of this erosion.

Along the coast is a lowland area, which, at its widest point, extends about 100 miles (160 km) inland. Between this lowland and the main plateau is an intermediate area, known as the subplateau, with a width from 14 miles (23 km) in the south to around 286 miles (460 km) in the north.

From the eastern side of this plain the land gradually rises toward the large plateau that occupies all but one third of the country's total area. In places in the south of the country, however, the change from the subplateau to the plateau occurs abruptly, and there are dramatic escarpments of up to 3,280 feet (1,000 m) in height.

Angola's topography includes some very rugged and inhospitable landscapes.

Nearly all of Angola's land is savanna—a grassy plain with scattered trees. The Cabinda enclave has a small area of rainforest, and in the deep southwest, near the border with Namibia, is a stretch of desert. This desert is called the Moçâmedes Desert and it forms the northern tip of the Namib Desert of Namibia.

From the Atlantic Ocean in the west, the desert gradually ascends to a semiarid plain where African ironwood trees grow. Few people live in the desert; communities are mostly found in small fishing towns on the coast. The unique tumboa (*Welwitschia mirabilis*), a desert plant with a short, wide trunk and two gigantic leaves that can survive for about 100 years, is found in this desert.

Savanna-covered hillocks.

The town of
Namibe on the
southern coast
receives less than 2
inches (5 cm) of
rainfall annually.

THE TUMBOA

The tumboa (*Welwitschia mirabilis*) is one of the most unusual plants in
the world. Found only in the Moçâmedes Desert in the south of Angola,
near the border with Namibia, it grows in the coastal area to about 150
miles (241 km) inland. The tumboa has only two large leaves that grow
throughout the life of the plant, which averages about 100 years.

The leaves grow to about 10 feet (3 m). Further growth is restricted
because when the tips of the leaves drop downward and touch the hot
sand, the leaves will die. As there is very little water in the desert, it is a
mystery how the tumboa obtains the water it needs to survive. The male
and female flowers are carried in cones that grow in a ring above the leaves.

PROVINCES

Angola is divided into 18 provinces that range in size from the small enclave of Cabinda in the north, about 31 miles (50 km) wide and 93 miles (150 km) long, to the vast Kuando Kubango in the southeast that is nearly 435 miles (700 km) wide.

The northern region of the country, made up of the three provinces of Cabinda, Zaire, and Uíge, has a typical landscape of tropical savanna. There are also areas of woodland suitable for cash crops such as coffee, cotton, palm oil, and sugar. Fish, both in the rivers and offshore, are a rich resource. The tsetse fly—known for transmitting disease—is common in the northern region, so raising cattle is uneconomical.

To the south is a region centered around Luanda and its neighboring provinces. This is fairly rich agricultural land, with plenty of timber in Bengo province. The richest agricultural land, though, is found in the central highlands region that covers the provinces of Huambo, Bié, and Huíla. There, a variety of crops can be grown, from corn and cassava for consumption to coffee and tobacco for cash sale.

The two coastal provinces in the southwest, Benguela and Namibe, have a dryer climate and do not support much agriculture, though

12

some cattle is raised. Similarly the inland provinces of Cunene and Kuando Kubango have an arid climate that makes agriculture difficult; raising cattle is the main activity. Finally, there are the eastern, inland provinces of Moxico, Lunda Norte, and Lunda Sul. They are characterized by open countryside and, in the northeast, rich deposits of diamonds and other minerals.

FAUNA

Angola's rich animal life includes leopards, lions, hyenas, elephants, hippopotamuses, giraffes, zebras, buffaloes, antelopes, and monkeys. Birdlife and reptiles, such as crocodiles, are also abundant.

A river flows through Kwanza Sul province.

Opposite: **A waterfall in Malanje province.**

The Cuanza is the longest river flowing entirely within Angola.

RIVERS

The three most important rivers in Angola are the Cuanza, 596 miles (960 km) long; the Cunene, 587 miles (945 km) long; and the Congo, which forms part of the border with the Democratic Republic of Congo. The Cuanza flows into the Atlantic Ocean about 40 miles (64 km) south of Luanda. Only the Cuanza and the Congo rivers are navigable for more than a short distance.

Several other rivers and their tributaries run across the country. Together, the rivers form an important potential source of hydroelectric power. Much of Angola's electricity is generated by dams on the Cuanza, Cunene, Catumbela, and Dande rivers.

CITIES

Luanda, situated on the northwest coast, is the capital of Angola. Founded in the 16th century, Luanda is also the country's largest city. Other important towns in the north are Cabinda, Soyo, Caxito, and Malanje. The most important urban centers in the central highlands are Huambo and Kuito. On the coast in the south, Benguela is the major town, followed by Namibe farther south. Other urban centers on the coast include Lobito and Tombua.

Inland, the population is low and towns are located near a source of water, with Menongue being one of the few urban centers. In the eastern inland region the important towns are Luena, Saurimo, and Lucapa.

A bird's eye view of Luanda's waterfront.

A diamond mine in Lunda Norte province. The alluvial soil here is rich with diamonds.

NATURAL RESOURCES

Angola's two most precious natural resources are oil and diamonds. The oil is mostly produced in the northern enclave of Cabinda, where most foreign oil companies are located. In recent years, however, substantial reserves of oil have also been discovered offshore, both in shallow and deep waters. There is now only one oil refinery in the country, but with plans for a second one, Angola could develop into one of the most important suppliers of refined petroleum in Africa. Oil accounts for about 90% of the country's total exports.

Angola is also an important supplier of diamonds for the world market, producing nearly two million carats of diamonds every year. It is believed that many new reserves have yet to be discovered. Angola has several relatively unexplored kimberlite (named after the famous diamond-producing Kimberley area of South Africa) regions that contain the type of volcanic rock that is a source of the gemstones.

Other natural resources include zinc and copper, although whether the reserves are large enough to be profitable over the long term is uncertain. An international mining company is now surveying the southwest of the country to determine the extent of these zinc and copper reserves. Angola is also believed to hold important deposits of gold, lead, and natural gas. Potential also exists for Angola to become an exporter of electricity because of the country's many rivers.

Angola's oil reserves have been estimated at 5.4 billion barrels (end-1996). It also has natural gas reserves estimated at over 65 billion cubic yards (50 billion cubic meters).

THE UPS AND DOWNS OF OIL

Angola depends heavily on oil for economic survival. The country is the largest oil producer in southern Africa, with current production reaching one million barrels per day. It has been estimated that the revenue earned could triple within 20 years with the new technology available for offshore drilling.

Much of the country's oil lies in the ocean's depths, over 3,280 feet (1,000 m) deep in places, and it is only recently that advanced drilling techniques have been developed that can exploit these deposits. In 1996 alone, nine new oilfields came into operation. Almost three quarters of Angola's oil is exported to the United States. However, the downside to this promising scenario is that the price of oil can go down as well as up. A sharp decline in the price of oil could seriously damage the economy of a poor country like Angola that depends overwhelmingly on oil as its chief source of foreign exchange.

HISTORY

THE HISTORY OF ANGOLA can be broadly divided into three stages: early history, before the first arrival of Europeans; the arrival of the Portuguese in the 15th century and subsequent developments; and more recent history, with its tragic events and the present status quo. Recent Angolan history, especially the years after independence in 1975, has been dominated by a civil war that has left hundreds of thousands of people dead and many more homeless.

The power struggle in the country was made worse by other more powerful countries taking sides, hoping to use the Angolan civil war to achieve their own objectives. The United States, the Soviet Union, and South Africa armed and supported the different groups that they thought would support their own interests. But no one side has managed to achieve complete victory and the civil war exacted a heavy toll on the Angolan people.

Opposite: **Victorious Angolan soldiers pose beside a legacy of Portuguese colonial rule in 1975.**

Left: **Popular Movement for the Liberation of Angola (MPLA) supporters in Luanda. MPLA dominates the Angolan government today.**

EARLY HISTORY

The land that is now Angola was inhabited from as early as 7000 B.C. by hunters and gatherers as well as settled communities of fishermen. The early hunter-gatherers, known variously as Bushmen, Khosian, or San, may have developed an elementary knowledge of iron-making. Iron technology originated in the Middle East and was introduced into north Africa by way of the Mediterranean. The art of smelting iron is believed to have worked its way down the west side of Africa around 300 B.C. through ancient trade routes across the Sahara Desert.

How and when farming and the use of iron tools developed in Angola and other parts of southern Africa remains uncertain. What is certain, however, is that the migration of Bantu-speaking people south to modern Angola had a decisive influence on future developments. The Bantu

Typical village life more than a hundred years ago in northern Angola, near the Congo river.

people, who probably came from what is now Cameroon, had an advanced knowledge of iron-making, which would have given them a great advantage over the Bushmen.

The migration of Bantu-speaking people into Angola may have begun as early as A.D. 500, but it occurred gradually over a period of time. There was also a later migration of Bantu speakers to Angola from eastern Africa. Much later, in the 14th century, another large movement of people to Angola took place. By the beginning of the 16th century nearly all of Angola was populated by Bantu speakers.

Ivory was a much sought-after commodity in trade between the African kingdoms.

KINGDOM OF KONGO

Very little is known about the history of the region after the first arrival in southern Africa of Bantu-speaking people. As farming developed some family groups may have achieved positions of power based on their ownership of cattle. This was probably the origin of the various kingdoms that arose after A.D. 1000. By 1200 the most powerful of these kingdoms was the kingdom of Kongo, which controlled a large area that included modern Angola. To the south of this kingdom a smaller kingdom known as the Ndongo kingdom, which stretched inland from Luanda as far as the Lucala River, also developed. Another kingdom, the Matamba kingdom, was based to the west of the Cuango River.

The Kongo kingdom's success was based on its people's skill in developing metal-working and pottery. The technique of weaving cloth from raffia palm became a sophisticated art, and Kongo cloth was traded as far west as the Atlantic coast in exchange for salt. The Kongo kingdom

Early trade in Angola. Many Europeans were attracted to Angola and other African countries by the profits that could be made from trade with the local population.

developed a currency based on sea shells, which it also obtained in exchange for its cloth.

These kingdoms jealously guarded their territories, which were usually defined by the natural course of rivers. Sometimes they interacted with one another—in the first half of the 16th century both the Matamba and Ndongo kingdoms paid tribute to the mightier Kongo kingdom in recognition of its superior power.

However, the arrival of Portuguese explorers and traders in the late 15th century was to fundamentally affect all the kingdoms. At first they quarreled among themselves over the benefits they thought they could gain by dealing with the Portuguese. Eventually, they united against the Europeans when they realized that the Portuguese were not merely interested in trade.

LUNDA KINGDOM

Besides the Kongo, there were also other powerful kingdoms. One of the most important was the Lunda kingdom that developed in the 16th century. Lunda was a village-based kingdom whose people lived as farmers and supplemented their food supply by hunting and fishing. The leaders of this kingdom originated in an area southeast of the present-day Democratic Republic of Congo and ruled through local chiefs who paid tribute to the king. The Lunda king was careful to appoint "advisers" in each of the chiefs' villages. These advisers ensured that the taxes that were due to him were collected.

The Lunda king was given the title of Mwata Yamvo ("The Lord of Vipers") and Lunda territory continued to grow in the 17th century. The people of the Lunda kingdom benefited from the planting of new crops from America that were acquired indirectly from the Portuguese. Corn was introduced in this way. So too was cassava, which was especially valued because of its ability to withstand periods of drought and still produce a good crop. With new food sources the Lunda empire expanded. Trade with the Portuguese developed, with ivory and slaves exchanged for guns and cloth.

SLAVERY

Slavery existed in Africa before the arrival of the Europeans. However, in terms of numbers, the organized transportation of slaves overseas, and the consequences for African society, nations such as Britain and Portugal completely transformed the activity. When the Portuguese first established themselves along the Cuanza River their main objective was to collect slaves. Over time this developed into a large-scale operation. Portugal's colony in Brazil needed a large number of slaves to work on the plantations. Between 1534 and the abolition of slavery in 1834 some four million Angolans were transported to South America.

Painting of an early Portuguese explorer.

THE PORTUGUESE

In the 1480s the Portuguese began arriving on the shores of Angola. Their first contact was with the king of the Kongo, and early relations between the two groups were friendly. Both sides had something to offer and mutual trade was easily established, with the Kongo king happy to exchange some of his slaves in return for the guns that the Portuguese brought with them.

The Ndongo kingdom was also eager to trade with the Europeans, and by the 1540s they were dealing with the Portuguese, who had established a coastal trading post at Luanda. They even invited some of the Portuguese leaders to their capital and then kept some of them there against their will, hoping to secure the best possible terms for future trade. This caused friction with the Kongo kingdom, who wanted to monopolize trade with the Europeans. Fighting broke out between the two African kingdoms; by 1557 the Ndongo had broken away completely from the Kongo.

By the 1570s, however, the Portuguese, spurred on by stories of fabulous gold deposits in the region, decided to take over the territory. In 1575 the Portuguese landed in force at Luanda where they established a military post. Their fort would become the first building in what would later develop into the capital city of Angola. At the time, though, their priority was the conquest of the interior, and in 1579 they were ready to move up the Cuanza River and attack the Ndongo capital.

A sketch of a Portuguese hunter and his attendants with a crocodile in the late 19th century.

COLONIZATION

The Ndongo resisted the advance of the invaders as best they could. It took the Portuguese four years to secure land on either side of the Cuanza River and establish a second military base at Massangano. This would become the main interior post for the collection of slaves before they were brought downriver to the coast and shipped across the Atlantic. The land they conquered was the beginning of what would later become the Portuguese colony of Angola.

The determination of the Portuguese to maintain a permanent presence in the region also brought them into conflict with the Matamba. The Kongo kingdom too changed its attitude toward the Europeans, and by the end of the 16th century all three kingdoms had joined forces against the common enemy. Between them they managed to halt the colonizing forces.

In 1912 the first diamond mines were established in Angola by the Portuguese.

This success was due in no small part to a new female leader of the Ndongo kingdom called Nzinga. Under Nzinga, the colonial advance was resisted and contained, but the Portuguese presence could not be removed. A treaty was made in 1684 that lasted until the middle of the 18th century. By then the Portuguese were ready to conquer more territory and they mounted a successful invasion of Matamba territory.

During the 19th century they strengthened their hold over the country and established cotton, rubber, and coffee plantations. Slavery had been abolished in 1834, but forced labor was still permitted, so for the Angolans little had changed since the days of slavery. By 1920 the country was declared "pacified," with all effective resistance over. The country was now a full-fledged colony with a civil administration.

QUEEN NZINGA

In the early struggle against the colonizing Portuguese, Queen Nzinga (1582–1663) emerged as the leader most able to resist the advance of the Europeans. In 1624 she became the queen of the Ndongo kingdom. She had negotiated a treaty with the Portuguese a year earlier and was not prepared to let them overstep the terms of the treaty.

When it became obvious that the slave-gathering Portuguese were not going to be bound by the treaty, she retaliated by offering refuge to slaves who had escaped from their territory. Her willingness to encourage revolt among Africans led to a Portuguese attack.

In 1626 she was driven out and replaced by a Ndongo ruler more willing to work with the Europeans. Nzinga, however, escaped to Matamba where she became their queen and continued to organize resistance. By 1635 she had developed an effective anti-Portuguese coalition and successfully contained their advance.

INDEPENDENCE MOVEMENTS

In the 1950s, Portuguese settlers began taking over the best farm land and expelling the Africans who had been working the land. Angolans were pressed to work on Portuguese plantations. It was under these conditions that nationalist sentiment in Angola began to develop. The first movement to emerge was the Popular Movement for the Liberation of Angola (MPLA). By the 1960s it had developed a guerrilla force and was receiving aid from the Soviet Union.

The second movement to emerge was the National Front for the Liberation of Angola (FNLA), which was based in the Democratic Republic of Congo (called Zaire at the time) and received aid from the United States. Later, in 1966, a splinter group from the FNLA formed the National Union for the Total Independence of Angola (UNITA).

Portuguese soldiers attempt to quell proindependence guerilla forces in 1961.

THE END OF COLONIAL RULE

Before independence was granted in 1975 there was terrible loss of life in Angola. Hundreds of Portuguese settlers were killed and 20,000 Angolans lost their lives.

The Portuguese colony of Angola came to an end as a result of a coup in Portugal in 1974 that overthrew the country's military government. The new government was intent on disowning its overseas colonies, and independence was granted to Angola in 1975. By the end of 1975, 300,000 Portuguese had left Angola; many deliberately destroyed factories and plantations before they left.

Unfortunately, independence was only the beginning of a new chapter in Angola's struggle to survive. The three nationalist movements, MPLA, FNLA, and UNITA, began jostling for power and civil war broke out.

Most Portuguese settlers fled Angola when the country gained independence in 1975.

CIVIL WAR

The civil war that has been a feature of much of Angolan life since 1975 owes much to the international conflicts of the time. The United States supported the FNLA and UNITA because they saw the struggle as a means of containing Soviet influence in Africa. South Africa, on the other hand, viewed the struggle as a way of resisting radical black nationalism.

South Africa, which had its own colony of Namibia bordering Angola, wanted to prevent the MPLA from gaining victory because the MPLA supported the Namibian struggle for independence. These outside forces were already involved in Angola before independence was granted in 1975. In 1975 Cuba joined the conflict and sent troops to support the MPLA against South African troops that had invaded from the south.

MPLA troops undergo training.

29

AN UNEASY PEACE

The Angolan civil war dragged on through the 1980s. At one point the MPLA commanded the support of most of the population, but because of their anticapitalist stand, the United States was determined to help UNITA defeat them militarily. This led to American support for a second South African invasion in 1981. However, South Africa withdrew from the conflict at the end of the 1980s. This was followed by the withdrawal of Cuban troops. With the collapse of the Soviet Union in the early 1990s, Soviet support for the MPLA stopped. The MPLA then began to shed its belief in Soviet-style economics and one-party rule.

A treaty was signed in 1991 between MPLA and UNITA and a new order seemed to be emerging with the promise of free elections and free speech. However, there was a return to civil war when UNITA, unhappy at losing

Angola's representative Afonso Van-Dunem addresses the assembly at the United Nations headquarters in New York in 1988.

Children march with the MPLA flag.

the elections that took place in 1992, took up arms again. Another peace treaty was signed in 1994, with the United Nations taking on the task of monitoring the cease-fire and demilitarization. The average Angolan yearns for peace, but the process of reconciliation is proving painfully slow.

THE FUTURE

United Nations troops and observers are still in Angola. The peace treaty of 1994, known as the Lusaka Protocol after the Zambian capital where the deal was brokered, still holds. The best chance for peace comes from a realization on the part of UNITA that it cannot win by force. Hopefully, when the next round of elections takes place, there will not be a return to the fighting that has cost so many Angolan lives.

GOVERNMENT

IN 1997, WHEN MOBUTU SESE SEKO OF ZAIRE was overthrown and Zaire renamed the Democratic Republic of Congo, hopes for peace in Angola were rekindled. Mobutu had been a staunch supporter of UNITA. The new government, on the other hand, supported the MPLA-dominated government of Angola.

In April 1997 UNITA joined the MPLA to form a new government, the Government of Unity and National Reconciliation. A few months later the people's assembly that was first elected in 1992 began functioning and for the first time representatives from both parties sat together in the National Assembly.

What were once important political differences between the MPLA and UNITA have become less clear-cut in recent years. The two parties can no longer be labeled simply as pro-West (UNITA) or anti-West (MPLA). The Cold War that dominated the international political stage after the end of

Opposite and left: **Over the last few decades, soldiers and guns have become the most potent form of power in Angola.**

World War II is now over. Moreover, the MPLA no longer believes in one-party rule and a centralized economy. But because the two parties have their origins in different parts of the country, and because they continue to appeal to different ethnic groups, there are still important differences that need to be overcome if Angola is to emerge as a united and peaceful country.

WHO RUNS ANGOLA?

In 1992, after elections that saw the defeat of UNITA, the army forces loyal to UNITA should have disbanded. But they withdrew to the northeast of the country instead, near the border with Zaire and close to the diamond-rich region. The right to rule Angola was again contested by two parties, and because the diamond mines provided UNITA with substantial wealth, the country was run by two separate governments, each with its own army.

THE PRESIDENT

The president of Angola is José Eduardo dos Santos. He is also the leader of the MPLA. He was born in 1942 into a Mbundu family. The son of a bricklayer, he joined the MPLA before he was 20 years old.

He studied engineering in the Soviet Union and when he returned to Angola joined the war of independence. He became president of the MPLA in 1979 and won the general election for president in 1992.

This uneasy situation lasted until 1997 when UNITA leaders met with officials from the United Nations and agreed to send its 70 deputies to Luanda to take their seats in the new National Assembly. The National Assembly is dominated by representatives of the MPLA because the MPLA won the majority of seats in the 1992 elections. UNITA, led by Jonas Savimbi, is now the official opposition party. Five smaller parties are also represented in the National Assembly. The prime minister is the head of the government, and this post is currently held by Fernando Franca Van-Dunem. UNITA has four ministers serving in Angola's current government. Executive power rests with the president, who is the head of state and commander-in-chief of the Angolan armed forces.

A soldier stands between two abandoned tanks.

Government buildings in Luanda.

THE COUNCIL OF MINISTERS

The chief administrative and executive organization in the government of Angola is the Council of Ministers. It is composed of the president and the ministers in charge of the various departments of government—defense, interior, foreign affairs, territorial administration, finance, economic planning, petroleum, industry, agriculture and rural development, fisheries, geology and mines, public works and urbanization, transportation, trade, health, education, assistance and social reintegration, culture, youth and sports, justice, public administration, employment, and social welfare, information, science and technology, posts and telecommunications, women's affairs, war veterans, hotels and tourism, and energy and water.

MPLA

MPLA stands for the Movimento Popular de Libertação de Angola (Popular Movement for the Liberation of Angola). Formed in 1956 under the

Angola's national anthem is "O Patria nunca mais esqueceremos" ("Oh Fatherland, never shall we forget").

KEEPING THE PEACE

The new government realizes that the chances of civil war erupting again will be greatly reduced if the UNITA army is dismantled. The government army is also too large for a peacetime government and needs to be reduced. Altogether, about 75,000 troops need to be demobilized, but this is not an easy task. A large amount of money is needed to provide the soldiers and their dependents with some alternative means of making a living.

leadership of António Agostinho Neto, it was the first political group to seek independence from Portugal. Support for the party came mainly from the Mbundu people, and the MPLA largely developed in Luanda and other large towns.

Both the MPLA and UNITA were nationalist parties that called for independence from Portugal, but there was an important political difference between the two groups. The MPLA was attracted to communism as an alternative to capitalism.

UNITA, on the other hand, was seen as an anticommunist party. It was this crucial difference in political ideology that led to the United States and South Africa throwing their support behind UNITA, and to Cuba siding with the MPLA.

In the 1980s the MPLA developed into a tightly-controlled party that sought to govern Angola through one-party rule. Corruption became a feature of the party, and people of Ovimbundu origin found it very difficult to obtain official positions, even if they were the most qualified. In the early 1990s the MPLA abandoned its Marxist past in favor of democratic socialism and endorsed multiparty elections in the wake of a peace settlement with UNITA.

MPLA supporters campaign for the party in the 1992 elections.

JONAS SAVIMBI

Jonas Savimbi, the founder of UNITA, was born in 1934. His father worked on the railways under the Portuguese and this helped Savimbi to attend both elementary and secondary school. Savimbi won a scholarship to study medicine in Portugal and he gradually become more interested in politics. In 1966 he established UNITA and built up its support in eastern and southern Angola among the Ovimbundu people. When an MPLA government was established in 1975, Savimbi organized military resistance, and with substantial help from South Africa and the United States, UNITA launched a civil war.

Jonas Savimbi (wearing red scarf).

UNITA followers in a show of support for the party.

Savimbi became the most well-known figure in Angolan politics during the 1980s. His fluent English and support from the United States helped establish his presence on the international stage. However, Savimbi is held to be largely responsible for the continuation of a civil war that has torn Angola apart and inflicted a terrible loss of life. After losing the democratic elections in 1992, he refused to accept the result and restarted the civil war. He continues to dominate UNITA, the result of a personality cult built up through the 1980s.

GOVERNMENT FROM THE OUTSIDE

The MPLA government, with a majority of seats in the National Assembly, is officially responsible for running the country. International organizations, however, play a vital role in Angola's development from a deeply-divided

THE GENERAL ELECTION OF 1992

The general election in 1992 was a major event in the government of Angola. Over 90% of registered voters turned out to vote, and some 400 international observers concluded that the election was fair and free, a view accepted by the United Nations and other international organizations.

The MPLA won nearly 54% of the votes, while UNITA obtained 34%. In the election for president the MPLA candidate, José Eduardo dos Santos, won 49.6%, while Jonas Savimbi of UNITA received 40%.

Angola's national flag consists of two colors in horizontal bands. The upper band is bright red and the lower one black. The bright red band represents the blood shed by Angolans during colonial oppression, the national liberation struggle, and the defense of the country. The black band represents the African continent. In the center a composition in gold is formed by a segment of a cog wheel, a machete, and a star, symbolizing the country's wealth.

nation into a modern state governed on democratic principles. The most important of these organizations are the International Monetary Fund (IMF) and the World Bank. If the government makes changes to the national economy that are approved by these organizations, then Angola will benefit from massive IMF loans and the World Bank will agree not to call in hundreds of millions of dollars in loans that have been provided to Angola. The Angolan government is thus not the only authority making decisions about the future of the country.

ECONOMY

ANGOLA'S ECONOMY has, for a long time, depended on a few natural resources. Before the Portuguese arrived, the country exported slaves and ivory. After colonization the trade changed to that of valuable agricultural crops as well as diamonds and oil. But the income earned from these resources did not stay in the country. Instead, it was mostly transferred to Portuguese banks and very little benefit filtered down to the ordinary working people.

With independence, the country was plunged into civil war and the economy continued to be mismanaged. Governments sought to control economic life by reducing private enterprise and using central planning. This did not work; it only encouraged corruption and poor management. A new approach is now being tried to manage the economy, but it will be many years before the unfortunate legacy of the past is overcome.

Opposite: **A worker dries fish in the sun.**

Left: **A worker at a diamond mine.**

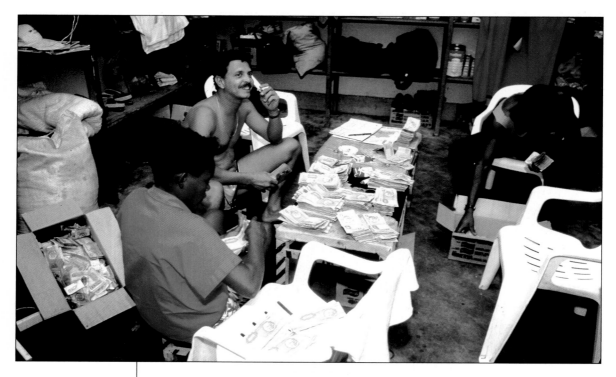

Store workers count the day's takings.

GALLOPING INFLATION

In recent years, inflation—the rate at which prices of goods and services increase over a fixed period of time—has been measured in the thousands. At the end of 1994 the annual rate of inflation was 2,000%, which meant that something that had cost the equivalent of a dollar at the beginning of the year was priced at a startling $2,000 just 12 months later. By the end of 1996 the rate had increased to 5,000%. During the five years between 1990 and 1995 the currency was devalued twice to help deal with galloping inflation.

On the first occasion the currency, the kwanza, was renamed the nova (new) kwanza at 1/1,000th of its former value. Five years later it was devalued again, with a similar reduction in its worth. Today, the currency is known once more as the kwanza. Skyrocketing inflation has important consequences for the country's economy and the lives of people. The present government hopes to reduce the rate of inflation to around 30% and some progress has been made.

SAVING: AN IMPOSSIBLE TASK

The ever-increasing rate of inflation has made it impossible to save money the conventional way—by depositing money in a bank and earning interest. The vast majority of Angolans do not use banks, and few banks exist, even in the capital city. It does not make sense to save money to spend the following month, partly because inflation lowers its value by the day and partly because most people struggle to survive on a day-to-day basis and there is rarely any money left over that could be saved. Those who are able to put some money away do so by exchanging their kwanzas for US dollars and moneychangers are a common sight on the streets of Luanda.

The Luanda gasworks.

WHERE DOES THE WEALTH GO?

Angola's annual gross domestic product is about US$9 billion. Most of this income is earned through the sale of oil and diamonds. The production of oil is essential to the country's economic well-being. The sale of oil accounts for over four-fifths of government revenue. A large proportion of this wealth is used to buy weapons.

Another 25% of national income is used to import the food that arrives daily at the port of Luanda. Without these imports the millions of inhabitants of Luanda and the other large towns would not be able to survive.

The political history of Angola has resulted in a poor country that is unable to directly exploit its own sources of wealth. Although there is a state mining company, only foreign companies with the necessary capital and technical skills are able to drill for oil and extract the diamonds on a large and profitable scale. Foreign companies negotiate with the government for a license that gives them the right to operate in a specific area. For example, a Canadian mining company established operations in Angola after the peace process began in 1994, with plans to generate US$400,000 a day from the extraction of diamonds.

A NEW ECONOMY

In the past, the Portuguese colonial government and the civil war that followed, imposed artificial conditions on the Angolan economy. Now for the first time Angola is largely able to structure its own economy, although international financial institutions retain an important say in the decisions that are being made.

An engineer plans operations at a diamond mine in Lunda Norte.

Since 1996 the government has privatized dozens of small- and medium-sized companies. Previously owned and run by the central government, these companies are being handed over to private companies that then become the legal owners of the business. The production of coffee is an example of this change. After independence the coffee industry was taken over by the government and over 30 different state-owned companies were formed. All these companies are now being sold to private investors.

In another important change, foreign banks are being invited to set up branches in Angola. Even Portuguese companies are returning to the country as private investors. The single largest investor in Angola is now

Women clean fish in Namibe province.

the United States, followed by France. Angola has also set out to recreate a healthy agricultural economy. Coffee and cotton plantations, both of which operated successfully under the Portuguese, are being reestablished.

The most important sector of the economy that is still supervised by the government is the diamond industry. Until very recently over three-quarters of this valuable industry was dominated by UNITA, which controlled the territory where most of the diamond reserves are located. Only three other countries in the world export more diamonds than Angola.

About 46% of Angola's workforce is female.

ANGOLA'S TRADING PARTNERS

Angola exports to:
> United States (64% of total exports)
> Belgium-Luxembourg (7%)
> China (5%)
> Portugal (4%)

Angola imports from:
> Portugal (53% of total imports)
> United States (9%)
> Spain (7%)
> France (5%)

Other important trading partners include the United Kingdom, Germany, Brazil, and the Netherlands.

Principal exports are oil and gas, diamonds, and coffee. Imports include oil equipment, vehicles and machinery, foodstuffs, textiles, and consumer goods.

AGRICULTURE

Angola's hopes of rebuilding the economy rest heavily on agriculture. The livelihood of three out of every four Angolans depends on the land, and yet less than 5% of agricultural land is cultivated today. Under Portuguese rule the Angolan agricultural economy was very successful, but it depended on the forced labor of Angolans and on management skills that the Portuguese did not pass on. When the Portuguese left, this system collapsed and, to compound difficulties, civil war broke out.

The obstacles that need to be overcome before a revival of Angola's agriculture can take place are enormous. Landmines will have to be removed from land suitable for growing crops or raising cattle. People who fled from war-torn rural areas will have to be persuaded to return to their farms. For that to happen, peace must be reestablished.

Women harvest corn in Kuando Kubango.

MANUFACTURING

The story of Angola's collapse as a manufacturing economy is a sad one. In 1973 manufacturing contributed 15% of the country's gross domestic product. By 1990 this figure had plummeted to around 5%.

Between 1960 and 1970 the light manufacturing industry grew steadily at around 10% a year. With independence, many of the skilled people running these industries returned to Portugal, and the government was forced to take over most of the companies without having the experience to run them efficiently. Decisions over such basic matters as the ordering of raw materials were made by a central government department that had little real understanding of the situation. As a result, between 1973 and the mid-1980s, the value of Angola's manufacturing production declined by over 50%.

Angola's potential to develop and boost its economy through manufacturing is enormous. Light industry has survived the war years in a variety of areas—textiles and clothing, footwear, soaps and detergents, and paint. There is also a basis for the manufacture of food in areas such as soft drinks, bakery products, and the brewing of beer.

A worker at a beer factory.

One of the most successful industries to have survived the ravages of the civil war is the cement industry. Overseas companies have invested jointly with the government and increasing profits demonstrate that there is tremendous scope for development. But until other light manufacturing industries are as successful, the country will be forced to import many products that could easily be manufactured in the country.

Luanda has a deep-water harbor that allows large ships to dock and unload their goods.

LUANDA—THE ECONOMIC HEART OF ANGOLA

The capital of Angola is the economic heart of the country. Every morning container ships unload their goods to the waiting traders in Luanda. What makes Luanda different from most major ports, however, is that the local economy largely operates through private individuals, overwhelmingly women, who do not form companies. A typical trader might be a woman with a small amount of capital who purchases a bale of cloth, which she then keeps at home. The cloth in the bale is then resold piece by piece for a small profit.

Over the past 30 years there has been little investment in Luanda. As a result the economic infrastructure is very poor. In the old city center the asphalt streets are mostly free of potholes, but the farther one travels outside the city, the more often potholes are encountered, and the bigger they are. In the shantytowns, or *musseques* ("MUS-seeks"), the roads are not surfaced, and after periods of rain are almost impassable to vehicles.

BUYING AND SELLING

The economy in Luanda and other Angolan towns operates on the basis of *compra e venda* ("COM-pra a VEN-dar," buy and sell). For example, a common means of livelihood for women in Luanda is to buy a bottle of cooking gas from one of the shops near the city refinery and then resell it at a higher price by the side of a road outside a marketplace. The profit earned from each bottle of gas sold may not be much, but a woman is happy to sell three bottles a day.

After selling one bottle—and on some days that may happen only once or not at all—the woman returns to the shop near the refinery with the empty bottle and has it refilled before returning to the same place by the roadside. Other items commonly bought and resold under this system include cigarettes, peanuts, canned milk, sugar, and other foodstuffs.

Cloth vendors at a large open-air market on the outskirts of Luanda.

TRANSPORTATION

The Portuguese colonial rulers developed transportation networks in the country by building railways and roads to help move produce bound for Europe. The most important railway line, known as the Benguela Railway, linked Angola with Zambia and the Democratic Republic of Congo. As a result of the civil war, the line has fallen into disuse. Only small sections are still in working order.

The second important line was in the south of the country and connected the town of Namibe with the iron-ore mining areas. This too has mostly fallen into disuse. Smaller railway lines have suffered the same fate, and until a major program of investment and repair gets under way, Angola's economy will be at a disadvantage.

The main highway in Angola runs north to south. Today the road system across the country covers some 46,500 miles (75,000 km). About one in 10 miles is surfaced with asphalt, while a similar proportion has a gravel surface. The remaining 80% of Angola's roads are unsurfaced dirt roads, which, like the railway lines, have received little maintenance over the last few decades.

During the 1980s and the early 1990s it was very dangerous to travel by road. Convoys were about the only way to transport goods safely across the country. A problem that has not been completely dealt with is the danger of mined roads. Although many of the major roads are now passable, it will be well into the 21st century before the mines are removed from all the smaller roads and they are safe for travel.

Obtaining spare parts for vehicles is still a problem, even in areas that were not directly affected by the armed conflict. Similarly affected is coastal transport, such as boats and small ships. Most ports are badly in need of repair and modern equipment. Internal air transport has become more and more important over the years, and there is now an extensive network of routes across the country.

The Benguela Railway.

ANGOLANS

THE LAST POPULATION CENSUS in 1970 recorded a population of just over five and a half million. The United Nations estimates the present population of Angola to be just under 13 million. This estimate is based partly on the electoral records drawn up for the 1992 elections and assumes a birth rate of 2.8% each year. By the year 2015 the population could almost double to 25 million people.

The birth rate is high compared to other developing countries in Africa, with women having an average of 6.6 children. However, given the size of the country, Angola still remains underpopulated, with an average density of only 26 people per square mile (10.2 people per square km). There are more women than men in Angola. This is especially true of younger people because the war has exacted a heavy toll on young men.

Opposite and left: **Angola's high birth rate means that young Angolans make up the majority of the population.**

A group of Portuguese
settlers.

DIVIDING A NATION

In Angola, a regional or tribal sense of identity is often more important
than the national sense. For example, someone's sense of identity as an
Ovimbundu could be far stronger and deeper than their sense of being
an Angolan. There are historical reasons for this—the Portuguese never
attempted to create a sense of national identity, and after independence
in 1975 the country was soon plunged into civil war, which pitted people
against each another along ethnic lines.

While the Portuguese did not adopt apartheid in the form it took in
South Africa, Europeans were treated as superior to the native inhabitants
of the country. Angolans—classified as "natives"—were only allowed to
hold menial jobs. They were obliged by law to carry special *caderneta*
("KAD-er-ne-ta," identity cards) that confirmed their status. As holders of
the *caderneta*, Angolans were subject to special laws and regulations that
limited their economic opportunities. In the 1950s, only 5% of "native"
children attended elementary or secondary schools and the vast majority

of older teenagers were unable to read or write. The only way for an Angolan to escape this fate was to learn Portuguese, turn their back on their traditional culture, and apply for the special status of *assimilado* ("ass-sim-ill-AD-o").

This was what many people from mixed African and European ancestry did. By the 1970s, there were about 30 Angolans of mixed blood for every hundred white Portuguese. Because most Portuguese colonists were male, those of mixed descent were likely to have a black mother and a white father. In practice, this also meant that these Angolans of mixed race tended to identify themselves with the white Portuguese rather than with the black majority.

Women of mixed race.

ETHNIC GROUPS

A member of the Ovimbundu tribe.

Angolans are members of various ethnic groups, and these groups tend to be concentrated in different parts of the country. Each group has its own language and shares a sense of common descent and a separate history—this is what works against a sense of national identity.

The largest ethnic group is the Ovimbundu, which makes up about 37% of the population and is mostly concentrated in the central highland areas covering the provinces of Huambo, Bié, Benguela, and northern Huíla. The most important subgroups of the Ovimbundu group are the Bailundu, Bieno, Dombe, Ganda, and Wambu. The Ovimbundu were important long-distance traders in the past, and although trade is still a traditional means of livelihood, the majority of Ovimbundu people are now engaged in agriculture.

The next largest ethnic group, representing about one in four Angolans, is the Mbundu people. There are three major subgroups—the Mbaka, the Ndongo, and the Dembos. The Mbundu people traditionally inhabit Luanda province, which includes the capital city of the same name. They have been exposed to the influence of the Portuguese more than any other ethnic group.

The people living in the northwest provinces of Zaire and Uíge belong mostly to the Bakongo group that is also found in the neighboring countries of Congo and the Democratic Republic of Congo. In Angola they make up about 15% of the population. The main subgroups of the

Bakongo group are the Bashikongo, Sosso, Pombo, Sonongo, and Zombo.

The main ethnic groups making up the rest of the population are the Lunda-Chokwe (8%) and the Nganguela (7%). As the name suggests, the Lunda-Chokwe live mostly in the provinces of Lunda Norte and Lunda Sul. The Nganguela people are scattered across most of the central provinces.

Another 6% of the population consists of the Nyaneka, Owambo, and Herero groups. The Nyaneka and Owambo are roughly equal in numbers, while the Herero comprise only 0.5% of Angolans. There are more Angolans of mixed white Portuguese and black African descent (about 2%) than there are Herero people. There is also a very small number of San and Khoi people, numbering little more than 5,000, living in the southern provinces of Cunene and Kuando Kubango.

The San live in the remote regions of the southern provinces.

CHOKWE

The Chokwe, a branch of the Lunda-Chokwe ethnic group, originally came from a highland region about 300 miles (500 km) southeast of Luanda. They were hunters, and when the Portuguese arrived they began to collect ivory and beeswax to exchange for guns. They formed groups up to a thousand strong and began to expand their territory to collect more ivory and beeswax. In this way they spread both to the north and to the east. In the 19th century, by which time there were few elephants left to hunt, the Chokwe became involved in the production of rubber because of the increasing European demand for this material. Chokwe women became adept at collecting the sap from the rubber trees that produced latex and rolling it into large hardened lumps that could be easily carried to the nearest trading post.

THE PORTUGUESE

Given that the Portuguese were in Angola for nearly 500 years one might think that a significant proportion of Angolans would be of Portuguese descent, but this is not the case. The history of their colonial rule makes up a large part of the explanation. Although they first arrived in 1480, it was not until the 19th century that the Portuguese established themselves in the plateau region of the interior. It was only in 1880 that northern Angola officially became a part of their colony.

For most of the 500 years, the Portuguese who lived in Angola tended to remain in a small number of coastal settlements. Even by 1940 there were only some 40,000 Portuguese living in Angola. Although there were 340,000 Portuguese in Angola at the time of independence, most of them had arrived between the mid-1950s and 1970. As the war of independence escalated in the 1970s, an increasing number of Portuguese chose to leave and return to Portugal, and this process was accelerated in the months following independence in 1975. Today, only a very small number of Portuguese still live in Angola, and they can nearly all be found in the capital city.

A DISPLACED PEOPLE

The civil war has greatly affected the lives of the people of Angola. Of the half a million people who are believed to have died in the war, some 90% were civilians. The war has also caused widespread suffering and reduced much of the population to extreme poverty. Over a million children are undernourished and over 50,000 have been orphaned by the war. There are also 50,000 disabled soldiers, and only a small minority of them have access to aids such as wheelchairs or artificial limbs. Thousands of Angolans have fled to neighboring countries in an attempt to escape the poverty. Today, although the country is more at peace than at any time over the last 30 years, hundreds of thousands Angolans still live as refugees in other countries.

Nearly half the population of Angola are refugees in another sense. Because the war has prevented so many people from growing their own food, they have been forced to leave the countryside and seek refuge in Luanda and other urban centers. These displaced people will not feel able to return to their homes in the countryside until the civil war is truly over and the roads have been cleared of landmines. In the meantime, the cities are becoming more congested and many of the inhabitants depend on humanitarian aid.

Refugee children at a feeding center run by UNICEF in Benguela province.

LIFESTYLE

SINCE 1961, WHEN THE FIRST WAVE OF REBELLION against colonial rule resulted in violent repression by the Portuguese, most Angolans have been profoundly affected by decades of strife and civil war. The United Nations has estimated the number of people killed in fighting at over half a million, with a similar number—mostly young children—dying from preventable diseases and malnutrition brought about by the civil war. Another two million people have lost their homes, and about 50,000 children have lost their parents.

The lifestyle of most Angolans is dictated by the constant struggle to find food and forge a livelihood in a country that periodically finds itself on the brink of collapse. In Luanda the average price of essential foods doubles every month, and ordinary people struggle to cope with this spiraling inflation. Even the supply of food and fuel is uncertain, and aspects of life that are taken for granted by many other societies—a regular

Opposite: **Two men in Kwanza Sul do their laundry.**

Left: **A bombed-out house in Ondjiva in Cunene province provides shelter for some Angolans.**

supply of water and electricity, for example—are difficult challenges that Angolans face every day. Over the years of civil war the number of people fleeing to the capital as a place of refuge has swelled. For many Angolans the daily struggle for existence is played out in the shantytowns that have grown around Luanda.

THE MUSSEQUES

The term "shantytown"—known as *musseque* in Luanda—describes a poor part of town, where people live in crudely built shacks. The term *musseque* comes from the words *mu* ("place") and *seke* ("sand"). The

In the *musseques*, home is usually a shack and amenities are scarce.

name is derived from the characteristic red sand found in coastal Luanda that forms the floor of the makeshift compounds that make up a *musseque*. About three million people, the majority of whom were not born in the city, live in the shantytowns of Luanda. Families fled to the capital city from their village communities in fear of their lives, and in the shanties where they now live they have a relative degree of safety.

Musseque dwellings are usually constructed around small compounds of about 270 square feet (25 square meters), with up to half a dozen single-story houses inside. The compound itself is usually surrounded by a wall of corrugated iron sheets or concrete blocks.

It has been estimated that in just three years between 1993 and 1996 the number of refugees and migrants setting up home in the capital increased by 20%.

LIFE IN A *MUSSEQUE*

The day begins at dawn. Often a woman starts the day's work by boiling water for coffee and breakfast. Clothes that have been left out to dry overnight need to be taken down and put away. The washing of clothes is a daily activity and clean garments are folded and kept in plastic bags in the living room. Water is always needed and this often involves a trip on foot with buckets to the nearest standpipe. Even then the supply is irregular and cannot be relied on. Some homes have access to a tank, holding 1,400 gallons (5,000 liters) or more of water, which is refilled by a tanker. The family washes each morning, using cold water, whatever the time of year.

Over half the population of Luanda's *musseques* are refugees. Most hope that one day they will be able to return to their village in the countryside where they were brought up. People who see Luanda as their permanent home are more likely to take part in one of the many self-help projects designed to improve the quality of life. Establishing running water and a regular supply of electricity, the proper disposal of garbage, and the provision of public toilets are all major concerns.

Residents of a suburb near Luanda collect water for their daily needs.

CITY LIFE

Many young people who travel to the nearest large town hoping to find employment and a better life are greatly disappointed. Life in a *musseque* is hard, and in Luanda, which attracts the majority of young people from the countryside, three quarters of the population live in extreme poverty. Jobs are scarce and there is always an urgent need to earn enough money to buy food. Obtaining fresh water is a constant problem. It has been estimated that the average family in the capital spends the equivalent of almost a day every week traveling to a source of fresh water, lining up for their turn, and then returning home. Poor families live on fish, because this is the cheapest way to feed themselves.

Street children who have been left to fend for themselves are a common sight in Luanda. They survive by begging for food and a few coins, and may be tempted into illegal activities. In recent years crime in the cities has increased significantly, with desperation driving some people to burglary, theft, and other more serious crimes.

RURAL LIFE

In rural areas most Angolans live in village communities. The typical family is an extended one, with grandparents and other relatives living with the parents and their children. Most children will only spend their younger years in the family home because the lure of the city is a powerful one, especially for young men. The city offers the possibility of employment and the chance to receive some form of education.

Angolans who live in the countryside depend on their farms for a livelihood. They may own some land, or a small group of families may rent a plot from the Ministry of Agriculture. The planting and harvesting of beans and cassava sustain many small farms. Toward the end of each year the fields are weeded and prepared for a new planting of crops. The December rainfall provides a good start to the new crop.

In many rural areas there are more women than men, and often this results in families being headed by a woman, who takes on the responsibility of looking after the family. This represents a significant change from traditional rural life, in which the male figure is the customary head of the family. But whether the woman is the head of the household or not, women usually do more work than men in the fields, looking after the crops and harvesting them.

Men are more likely to take charge of the family's cattle, following an age-old tradition across many parts of Africa. The average extended family may have a herd of about 20 cattle. Each year one or two may be sold for cash to buy necessities that the family cannot grow or produce themselves.

Another means for rural families to earn some extra cash is by working in traditional crafts, such as the making of household and kitchen items. There is always a demand for cooking utensils and farming tools, and many women earn a small but valuable income this way. For centuries, women in African societies have been associated with the making of pottery, and this is as true in Angola today as it was a millennium ago.

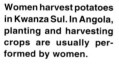

Women harvest potatoes in Kwanza Sul. In Angola, planting and harvesting crops are usually performed by women.

THE MARKET

In Luanda and other towns the local market is patronized by most families every day. A variety of produce is available and it is in the market that essential foodstuffs are bought. In the countryside, the local market may be a day's walk away, and villagers go to the market whenever they need to buy something or when they have some surplus food to sell.

Luanda's main market is the largest in the country and one of the largest in Africa. Every morning, shortly after dawn, over 50,000 traders descend on the marketplace with their stock of food and other items for sale. They arrive in trucks and cars of all sizes, packed to the brim with produce. Because of the large number of traders in the market, a mini-economy devoted to simply feeding all those who work there every day has sprung up.

The Luanda market is far more than just a food market. It is the African equivalent of a huge shopping mall where everything that a family might need may be found. Even in the 1980s, when the government tried to outlaw private economic activity, the Luanda market continued to operate as a huge black market.

For many of Luanda's poor, the market provides a living. One common practice is for people to buy produce inside the market and then try to resell it at a small profit at the side of a road outside the market. This is because the market itself is still regarded as a potentially dangerous place, and many people prefer to make their purchases from the side of a nearby street.

A fruit and vegetable market on the outskirts of Luanda.

EDUCATION

Most children will not attend school after the fourth grade of elementary school. Children who want to attend a secondary school often have to consider moving to Luanda or one of the larger towns. Schools in Luanda conduct up to three different sessions a day, with the first starting at 7 a.m., followed by a second session starting at 11 a.m., and a third school session from 3 p.m. to 7 p.m. The last session is usually for adults. Luanda schools are unusual because there are so many refugees in the city that the existing number of schools cannot accommodate those who want to attend with a single session or even two.

A classroom in Luanda. The best students may eventually go on to study at Angola's only university, the University of Luanda.

Children of secondary school age are expected to help out with family chores and sometimes their work at home prevents them from attending school regularly. Some women, for example, set up a small table by the door of their house that becomes a shop for whatever they have previously bought and are now trying to resell. Older children are sometimes expected to help run this "shop."

Teachers usually only teach one session each day, and although their wages are paid by the government, there is no money available for books or furniture. Students have to bring everything that is needed for the day's lesson and it is not unusual to see young students walking to school carrying a bench on their head. A typical classroom may have as many as 50 children.

Education between 7 and 15 years of age is provided free of charge by the government.

ASSIMILADO

Under Portuguese rule the Angolan people were classified as "natives" and were not allowed to enjoy the "benefits" of European civilization until they had undergone the process of *assimilado*, or assimilation. To be assimilated means to be absorbed into a larger group, and in Angola this meant an African had to abandon his or her traditional culture and adopt European customs and habits.

Strict rules laid down the conditions: a minimum age of 18, fluency in the Portuguese language, a clean police record, and an occupation with a salary. Beyond these rules lay a clear understanding that an Angolan had to be prepared to turn his or her back on traditional village culture and adopt the manners and dress of the Portuguese. An Angolan had to apply to become an *assimilado* and, if successful, a special identity card was issued to show that the holder had successfully adopted a new cultural identity.

HEALTH

The low level of healthcare available and the poverty that affects most Angolans means that many children born in Angola never have an opportunity to grow up. For every 1,000 children born, about 170 will die before they reach the age of five.

In many other countries, children are immunized against infectious diseases that can prove fatal in their early years. In Angola, only about one in three children receives injections that protect them against diseases such as measles and polio. Most parents do not know the value of a simple vaccination because they have never been informed about it. The lack of healthcare centers, doctors, and trained nurses and midwives also means that for every mother who visits a hospital to give birth, another mother will deliver at home without even the help or advice of a midwife. Although reliable statistics are not available, it is believed that the number of mothers who die in childbirth in Angola is one of the highest in the world.

Under colonial rule, healthcare in Angola was mostly left to religious missions and, in the towns, to privately-run clinics. After independence the government took over the responsibility of providing its citizens with basic healthcare but failed to allocate sufficient funds. With the outbreak of civil war healthcare received even less priority. By the mid-1990s less than 3% of public expenditure was devoted to health. There are few doctors and nurses in Angola. Many are non-Angolans working in Luanda and are often employed in private clinics, which few of the poor can afford. While government-run clinics are available in Luanda, the lack of trained staff is a serious problem.

In rural areas people depend on clinics run by religious organizations. Many also still rely on traditional healers, who use spells and magical potions to rid the body of unhelpful spirits seen to be the cause of the problem. AIDS is also a growing threat.

Medical personnel promote healthcare in Kuando Kubango.

RELIGION

MANY ANGOLANS follow customary beliefs and practices that are usually called traditional religions. This is a broad term that is used to describe African religious beliefs that are not part of Christianity or Islam. A large portion of the population also profess to be Christian, mainly Roman Catholic. Unusually for an African nation, Angola has virtually no Muslim population. All religion was discouraged by the left-wing government in Luanda after independence in 1975. Religious institutions lost their schools, clinics, and properties. But when the MPLA abandoned communism, religious organizations regained influence, especially the Roman Catholic Church, which played an important role in securing national reconciliation.

Opposite: **The Nossa Senhora do Carmo Church in Luanda.**

Left: **Spiritual beliefs still play an important role in Angolan life today.**

THE LIVING DEAD

The term may sound like something from a horror movie, but it refers to the fundamental belief in Angola and other parts of Africa that the meaning of a person's life does not end with the death of their body. This belief is not the Christian idea of resurrection of the body or the notion that people will ultimately be judged according to their life on earth.

Nor is there a sense of heaven and hell. Even the idea of an all-powerful God—so central to both Islam and Christianity—is not linked to the tremendous reverence that a person may receive after their death. When someone dies they may be remembered by name for 100 years or more, the memory being passed down through three generations through word of mouth. A family shrine may even contain remnants of their bones.

Thus in a sense they remain a member of the family long after they have died. If a misfortune befalls a family member, the family may consult an expert in these matters—a "diviner," sometimes also called a witch doctor—to find out if the deceased person is unhappy about something. In Angola the diviner is known as the *kimbanda* ("kim-BAN-da").

DIVINATION

In Angolan society, a diviner is someone who uses special means to find out something about the world of the supernatural. In larger villages the diviner is a specialist who usually works with his own divination basket. The basket contains a number of small ritual objects, such as clay figurines, pieces of polished metal, carved pieces of bone, and the teeth or horns of animals.

Special prayers are made to the ancestors, and the diviner shakes up the basket as part of the ritual. Then the diviner studies the arrangement of the objects once they have settled and gives his interpretation. Many diviners also have a knowledge of herbal medicine.

Diviners are usually consulted when an individual has an illness or complaint of some kind that is thought to have a spiritual cause. The diviner hopes to identify the cause and remedy the problem by appropriate prayers. Some diviners specialize in certain illnesses, and the more respected a diviner is, the larger the fee they are able to charge for their services.

Opposite: **A religious symbol of the Chokwe people.**

NAIL FETISHES

A fetish is a term from anthropology—the study of cultures—for describing an object that is worshipped by a people because of a belief in the object's magical or spiritual quality. The Kongo people who live in northern Angola and southern Democratic Republic of Congo have fetish figures that are believed to be able to absorb, and hence render harmless, misfortunes brought about by evil spirits.

A person who feels he is the victim of an evil influence will stick nails in the fetish. Nail fetishes are sculptured from wood for this special purpose. Sometimes the figure is built with a space inside where magical medicines can be stored. The medicine, often made from local plants, is not used for bodily illnesses, but to remove the evil spirit that has afflicted the sufferer.

CHRISTIANITY

Christianity began in Angola with the arrival of the Portuguese toward the end of the 15th century. Their first contact inland was with the Kongo kingdom and it produced a difference of opinion within the kingdom on how best to deal with the European presence. Eventually the faction that wanted to encourage contact emerged victorious, with the help of the Portuguese, and in 1506 an early convert to Christianity seized the throne and became King Afonso I. He was the first African Christian to wield power in Angola and through his influence the new religion spread with the assistance of Portuguese priests.

In the late 19th and early 20th century, missionaries introduced Protestantism. Several Christian societies, including Protestant societies from North America, sent their missionaries to Africa and they eventually

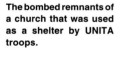

The bombed remnants of a church that was used as a shelter by UNITA troops.

reached Angola. Jonas Savimbi, the founder of UNITA, was a student at the school run by Canadian and US Congregationalists. Initially the process of conversion was slow and for a long time the missionary stations were confined to the coastal region. In the early 20th century, however, these missionaries began to make an impact. A major reason was that a missionary station often offered some elementary education and basic health services. Over time this attracted large numbers of people who had no other way of acquiring literacy or gaining access to healthcare.

Throughout the years of civil war, Christian churches were never banned outright. However the power of the Catholic Church diminished in the decade after independence, partly because the MPLA government did not want to encourage any organization that might rival its own power. Today Christian missions continue to operate in Angola.

Afonso I, the Kongo king of 1506–43, communicated with the Pope in Rome to announce his conversion to Christianity.

MISSIONARIES IN ANGOLA: GOOD OR BAD?

FOR: The missionaries established the first schools in Angola for the non-Portuguese. They needed converts who would agree to become Christian teachers. In return they offered free education. They performed a valuable role in opening the door for black Angolans to educate themselves. Missions also established a rudimentary health service that benefited many people.

AGAINST: The first missionaries in Angola actively supported the slave trade. They argued that they were saving the souls of the African godless. As late as 1870 a marble chair on the quayside at Luanda was reserved for the bishop who baptized Angolans in the hundreds as they were rowed by in chains on their way to the slave ships that would transport them across the Atlantic Ocean.

The missionaries who first spread Christianity in Angola did not understand or respect traditional African forms of belief. Their evangelical approach dismissed the religion they encountered as childish superstition. They worked to replace it with their own beliefs and also spread their cultural values. Traditional cultural practices were condemned by missionaries without understanding their role within African society.

LANGUAGE

THE OFFICIAL NATIONAL LANGUAGE OF ANGOLA is Portuguese. About 40% of the population learn and speak only this language. Other Angolans are brought up as a member of a particular ethnic group and learn to speak the language of that group as well as Portuguese. Many people do not learn to read or write their non-Portuguese African language. Indeed, before European colonization spread across Africa, the majority of cultures with their own languages did not have a written form.

Europeans often mistook the absence of a written language as evidence of underdevelopment, failing to understand that a culture can have a sophisticated form of communication capable of transmitting information across generations, without the need for a written form. In such cultures what is important is the oral tradition, and this is very true of Angolan society.

Opposite: **A young Angolan with an election placard in Portuguese.**

Left: **Pro-MPLA graffiti in Luanda.**

Angolans at a roadside stall. Angolan oral tradition includes many folk tales that feature slow-thinking bears and cunning, quick-witted rabbits.

ORAL TRADITION

In the mid-1970s, during the civil war, one faction arrived in a village and tried to gain the support of the villagers. The following story was told as a way of communicating with the people:

One day there was a rabbit who wanted to marry the daughter of a bear. The rabbit went to the bear and asked for his permission, but the bear refused and told the rabbit that only someone who could build a house in one day would be a suitable match for his beautiful daughter. The rabbit went away and gathered from his large family all the rabbits who looked like him. Then, making sure that the bear only ever saw one rabbit at any one time, they all worked together and succeeded in building a house in just one day. The bear, suitably impressed, gave permission to the clever rabbit to marry his daughter.

This story was readily understood by the villagers as a parable promoting the idea of working together for a common end because Angolans would have been taught in this manner from early childhood.

PORTUGUESE

Portuguese is the national language and more people speak Portuguese in Angola than in any other African nation. In the towns and cities, daily life is conducted using Portuguese. Only in rural areas do people use their ethnic African language regularly. Nevertheless, for well over half the population, Portuguese remains a second language.

Portuguese is still widely spoken today because of historical reasons. It was the language of the ruling class who colonized the country, leaving the various ethnic languages of Angolans relegated to an inferior role. The mother tongues of the ethnic groups were not acknowledged and were not used in any dealings between the colonial powers and the ordinary people. Any Angolan who wanted to receive an education and obtain a job outside of farming had little choice but to learn Portuguese.

The need for Angolans to learn Portuguese was an essential aspect of the *assimilado* process. A formal language test required an Angolan to show fluency in both speaking and writing Portuguese.

Workers learn to read and write Portuguese in the early days after independence. Adult literacy is about 43% in Angola today.

Some African words, like maka *("MAR-ka"), meaning "problem" and the local term for a diviner,* kimbanda, *have entered the Portuguese spoken in Angola.*

85

LANGUAGE GROUPS

As seen earlier, Angolans have a strong sense of ethnic and regional identity. A primary reason for this is because the different ethnic groups have their own languages. The Ovimbundu people, the largest group in the country, speak Umbundu—the language most commonly used and understood in central and southern Angola. Kimbundu, the language of the second largest ethnic group, the Mbundu, is spoken mainly in the provinces of Luanda, Kwanza Norte, and Malanje.

Historically, Luanda province is the area that has been most influenced by the Portuguese, and so not surprisingly, the legacy of colonization on

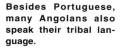

Besides Portuguese, many Angolans also speak their tribal language.

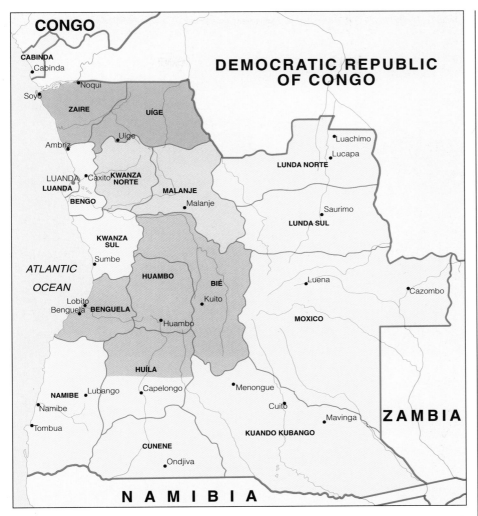

CONGO

CABINDA
•Cabinda

DEMOCRATIC REPUBLIC
OF CONGO

•Noqui
Soyo
ZAIRE   UÍGE

•Uíge
Ambriz

•Luachimo
•Lucapa
LUNDA NORTE

LUANDA •Caxito KWANZA
LUANDA   NORTE
BENGO

MALANJE
•Malanje

KWANZA
SUL

•Saurimo
LUNDA SUL

ATLANTIC
OCEAN

•Sumbe

HUAMBO   BIÉ
•Kuito

•Luena
MOXICO

•Cazombo

Lobito
Benguela BENGUELA
•Huambo

HUÍLA

NAMIBE •Lubango   •Capelongo
•Namibe
•Tombua

•Menongue
Cuito•

•Mavinga

ZAMBIA

CUNENE
•Ondjiva

KUANDO KUBANGO

N A M I B I A

**Main Languages
Spoken in Angola**

Umbundu

Kimbundu

Kikongo

language has been most keenly felt by the Mbundu. They generally speak Portuguese and, in many cases, the use of the European language is more prevalent than the native language.

In the northwest of Angola, in the provinces of Zaire and Uíge, the Kikongo language is spoken by the Bakongo people. This language is also spoken by people who belong to the same ethnic group in the neighboring countries of Congo and the Democratic Republic of Congo. There are also some small subgroups of Bakongo people living in Cabinda who also speak a dialect of Kikongo.

A television camera crew films an event. Introduced in 1976, Angola's television service broadcasts to some 63,000 receivers.

UMBUNDU

In its traditional form, Umbundu, the language of the Ovimbundu, employs various proverbs and sayings that are rooted in the lives of the people who speak the language. Two examples are expressions that translate as "We have roots in the fields of our ancestors" and "The advocate speaks, the king decides." In an Umbundu conversation the speaker who uses one of these sayings will do so within a particular context, and usually the person being spoken to would interpret the remark in the light of the context.

For example, if there was a disagreement about the ownership of a plot of land and someone made the remark about roots in the fields of ancestors, this might be understood in terms of a claim to ownership based on a family relationship. If the other speaker replied by quoting the remark about advocates and kings this might be understood as a way of saying that the matter needs to go to arbitration.

THE MEDIA

National dailies in Angola include *O Jornal de Angola* and *Diário da República*. *O Jornal de Angola*, founded in 1923, is published in Luanda and has a circulation of over 40,000. *Diário da República* (circulation: 8,500) is the official government bulletin. Regional newspapers are also published in several towns.

The state-owned Rádio Nacional de Angola broadcasts in Portuguese, English, French, Spanish, and several tribal languages, including Kimbundu, Umbundu, Kikongo, and Chokwe. There are about six million radio receivers in the country. A limited television service is operated by Televisao Popular de Angola.

A boy delivers newspapers in Luanda.

ARTS

POPULAR TRADITIONAL ART FORMS in Angola include sculpture, mask-making, and music and dance. These flourish alongside everyday art forms such as pottery and basketwork. At the individual level, Angolans express their artistic sense by creating beautiful hairstyles and headdresses that are usually decorated with a variety of adornments. Angolans also have a tradition of scarification, designed to enhance the visual beauty of the body.

SCULPTURE

Sculpture is one of Angola's oldest art forms, beginning with wood and ivory, but now also using metal as a base material. Originally, the designs

Opposite: **Angola's cultural heritage includes many forms of traditional dances.**

Left: **A musician heats a drum to tune it. The skin becomes stretched out as the drum is played.**

A throne sculpture from Angola's past.

that inspired sculptors had their origins in traditional religious beliefs and were often abstract in form. The arrival of Europeans in the 16th century exposed Angolans to Christian imagery, and this had an important influence on Angolan artists even after the decline of Catholicism in the 18th century.

Another important influence that still plays a part in contemporary Angolan sculpture has been European and North American interest in ethnic African art. This has had the effect of introducing non-African pictorial ideas as subjects for sculptors. For instance, a traditional subject often portrayed by Angolan artists is that of the disgruntled ancestor who bewails the fact that he has not been shown the proper respect by his living ancestors. Small carved objects of such figures are a familiar item in the diviner's basket of ritual objects.

Sazangwiyo, a Chokwe artist familiar with French sculptor Auguste Rodin's statue of "The Thinker," used the disgruntled ancestor figure to produce a modern African version of the famous image. Sazangwiyo's sculpture has become well known and is often imitated.

CHOKWE ART

Chokwe art is renowned for the quality of its wooden sculptures. The best examples were made between the 16th and mid-19th centuries, when the Chokwe were under Lunda rule. After 1860, the Chokwe rose up against the Lunda and even dominated them, but the sculpture of this period is not considered as good.

A feature common to Chokwe art is the large upturned hairstyles on figures, possibly a reflection of what was once a fashion among the leading chiefs and their families. Chokwe sculptures often portray their leaders with hands and feet on a clearly exaggerated scale—a pair of hands, for example, would be significantly larger than the figure's head. This signifies the great power and strength of the rulers.

ANGOLAN PAINTERS

In the second half of the 20th century, a number of Angolan artists have achieved international recognition for their paintings. One of the earliest and most famous is José zan Andrade, more familiarly known as Zan. He was born in 1946 and taught himself how to paint. He first became known for his work in Chinese ink painting and *gouache* ("gwash"), a method of painting that uses opaque pigments ground in water and mixed with a glue-like substance. Contemporaries of Zan, who have been influenced more by modern art movements, include Tomas Vista (born in 1957) and Paulo Jazz (born 1940).

The Chokwe people are also known for the quality of their weapons, some of which bear the fine decorative motifs used by woodcarvers.

MASK PAINTING

Mask painting brings together the art of sculpture and the art of painting. The mask itself is usually made of wood or by using a wicker frame and lining it with bark cloth. The cloth or wooden surface is then painted. Masks are used in rituals and ceremonies, such as those to mark the transition from childhood to adulthood and the celebration of a new harvest.

The start of the hunting season may also be marked by a mask ceremony, with some masks painted to represent the animals that the community hopes to hunt successfully.

WEAVING

The art of weaving first developed as a practical skill, mostly to produce mats for use in the home. When imported, machine-made textiles became more readily available, the art of weaving in Angola went into decline. Only recently, beginning in the 1980s, have Angolan women revitalized the art. Today, weaving has emerged as a specialized art that caters to an international market, although weavers still draw on traditional motifs for their designs and ideas. One of the most successful contemporary weavers is Maria Luiza da Silva, who first learned the skill of weaving from her family before going on to study the subject at art school. She works with wool and burlap, creating subtle and complex designs on tapestries.

Baskets from Huíla province woven from reeds.

SONG AND DANCE

Song, dance, and music are all fundamental aspects of traditional African culture. Regions that are widely separated geographically may have surprisingly similar forms of song and dance, and although no one has been able to explain these similarities, they presumably hark back to an earlier time when these art forms were being developed. For example, in parts of eastern Angola there is a form of multipart singing that uses exactly the same tone as that found among an ethnic group in Côte d'Ivoire in West Africa.

Nevertheless some forms of Angolan dance are unique to the country. In the southwest of Angola, for example, the Nkili dance uses a pair of

An all-male group sings and plays guitars.

dancers to very dramatic effect. At the climax of the dance the male dancer leaps into the air, landing with his hands on the shoulders of the female dancer, who balances him on her shoulders. Such a dance requires constant practice and strong shoulders on the part of the woman.

One attempt to understand and classify the great variety of African dance styles is based on the idea that different styles use different parts of the body. European dance, by comparison, is said to treat the body as a single whole. According to this system, many of the Angolan dance forms revolve around the movement of the pelvis to create a characteristic form.

Another category of Angolan dance is characterized by the use of masked dancers, who use a greater variety of movements. Each set of movements, using a particular part of the body, has its own name in the local language.

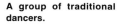

A group of traditional dancers.

MASKED DANCES

Dances based on the use of masks are fairly unique to west and west-central Africa. The region bounded by eastern Angola and parts of Zambia and the Democratic Republic of Congo is one of the richest sources of masked dancing in the continent. There is a wide variety of masks, and each ethnic group has its own colors and designs. Just as important is the function or meaning attached to a particular mask, because this helps to convey the story behind the mask or the significance associated with a specific mask.

Many of the Angolan masks represent ancestral members of a prestigious royal family. Some masks represent officials and servants of the court. Masked dances thus perform a similar function to oral tradition—they help preserve a sense of history and identity that is not dependent on books and writing. When performing a dance the person wearing the mask also uses gestures and pantomime-like actions to convey the character represented by the mask.

The Mbwela people distinguish two kinds of masked figures. The masks worn by men are known as the makisi avamala *("ma-KI-si a-va-MAR-la"), while the "mask of women" is called the* makisi avampwevo *("ma-KI-si a-vam-PWEV-o"). In reality, the women do not wear masks that cover their heads, but instead color their bodies with paint and only cover their hair.*

MUSICAL INSTRUMENTS

Angolan music is produced using a rich variety of traditional musical instruments. A typical example of a percussion instrument is the *saxi* ("SAR-ki"), more commonly known as maracas. In Angola these are made from the dried fruit known as *maboque* ("MA-boo-ker") and are filled with dried seeds or glass beads.

Drums, known as bongos or tam-tam, vary in size from one region to another, but they are often a popular instrument for accompanying dancing. In the past, these drums were used to send messages. Other traditional instruments include the *marimba* ("marr-IM-ba"), a type of xylophone, and the *xingufos* ("SING-U-fos"), which are large antelope horns, cleaned and dried.

A rare Angolan instrument is the *sagaya* ("sar-GA-ya") of the Humbi people in the southwest of the country. An ordinary hunting bow is fitted

DANCE OF THE NDZINGI

The Mbwela people celebrate in mask form the character of the ndzingi, a figure from Angolan folklore who lives far away from people in the forest. He is a giant and this is depicted in a grand mask with a huge head that is built up from a skeleton of wood that is then covered with barkcloth.

Ndzingi usually appears as a menacing figure who stomps and rages while threatening the audience with a bundle of twigs that he waves around him. Suddenly, and very dramatically, his behavior changes to represent a drunk-like figure, who tries to hold himself together before finally collapsing in a heap on the ground.

The audience laughs in relief at the spectacle of a giant whose head was too heavy for his own body.

with a mouth brace and the player breathes through the brace while stroking the bow's string with a fine twig-like strip of leather. As the player alters his breathing and the position of his mouth, the tone produced by playing the string changes.

Another more common string instrument is the *hungu* ("HUNG-go"). A small stick, held in the right hand, plays the bow, which is held at stomach level. The *hungu* was taken to Brazil in the days of slavery and it is now known in South America as the *berimbau* ("bur-IM-ba").

AGOSTINHO NETO

Agostinho Neto, the first president of independent Angola, was widely recognized as an accomplished poet. Born in 1922 in Bengo province, Neto studied medicine in Lisbon. He first became known at the age of 26 when he published a volume of poems and joined a national cultural movement aimed at rediscovering indigenous Angolan culture. Neto died in Moscow in 1979.

The following lines are taken from one of his poems, "Fire and Rhythm":

Rhythm in light
rhythm in color
rhythm in movement
rhythm in the bloody cracks of bare feet
rhythm on torn nails
Yet rhythm
rhythm.

Oh painful African voices.

Slavery exported African dance forms to both North and South America. The Brazilian dance known as the lunda, *is related to an Angolan dance. When it returned to Africa, it became one of Luanda's most popular dances. Now called the* masemba *("MASS-m-ba"), it is a type of belly dance, where a pair of dancers thrust their stomachs toward one another. The word* lunda *comes from a Bantu word* kilunda *("KILL-un-da"), meaning spirit, which suggests that the dance has its origin in a religious ritual.*

LEISURE

DEVASTATED BY DECADES OF CIVIL WAR, the people of Angola have had less opportunity to enjoy leisure time than people in many other parts of the world. Today as in the past, the family provides an emotional foundation for the enjoyment of leisure time. Leisure for many people is the informal social life of the home and the village community.

The years of civil war disrupted family life and forced many people to rely on themselves. The massive drift of population to Luanda and other urban centers has also caused overcrowding, widespread unemployment, and a general sense of insecurity.

Still, a determination to survive has characterized life in these difficult circumstances. Most families have been fragmented or traumatized by the war, but Angolans have still managed to find moments to come together and enjoy each other's company. This is part of the rebuilding of Angola.

Opposite: **Beach bathers against the backdrop of an oil rig.**

Left: **A local bar in southern Angola.**

The beach on Luanda island. Visitors can enjoy various activities, including swimming and beach games.

A DAY AT THE BEACH

Luanda has a beautiful, natural bay with a sandy beach. This bay was where the Portuguese first landed and where, in the centuries that followed, thousands of poor Portuguese arrived to start a new life in Africa. Today, the same beach is open to every one and provides relaxation and recreation for the poor of the city. On the weekend especially, the beach is crowded with families.

On one side of the bay is a narrow peninsula of land that stretches into the sea. On the weekends both sides of this peninsula are crowded with Angolans enjoying picnic lunches. During the week people also come to the beach to relax after work and to escape from the drudgery of shantytown life. A small island nearby attracts weekend visitors who are able to organize the boat ride there and back.

102

A MUSSEQUE *EVENING*

During the week, leisure time in a Luanda shantytown revolves around the evening meal. With family members leaving for work at different times, the evening meal is an occasion for everyone to come together and talk about their experiences during the day. The father may have some good news, even if it is only a rumor that new water pipes are going to be laid down or that the electricity station that used to provide power to the *musseque* is finally being repaired.

The mother may announce that she has sold more than the usual amount of food at the market that day. After the meal, oil lanterns and perhaps a fire in the yard outside will be lit. The family gathers around and continues their conversation; perhaps they are migrants in Luanda and some news has reached them about relatives still living in a part of the country controlled by UNITA forces. It is very difficult to travel to remote parts of the country, and there is no postal service.

Before going to bed, some chores may be completed—water may need to be collected for the morning, or wet clothes may need to be hung out to dry.

LEISURE IN THE COUNTRYSIDE

A traditional form of leisure in the countryside is for a small group of friends or neighbors to gather around an open fire, especially when a full moon provides plenty of light, and talk. An interesting or amusing story, perhaps first brought to the village by someone who has been working in Luanda, will be told more than once. A more traditional story may be told by one of the highly respected elders of the village. Sometimes, such a story is accompanied by someone playing a type of xylophone known as the *marimba* drum.

Battery-operated radios are found in many homes. Besides providing people with news, the regular music broadcasts are a source of pleasure for many.

The drum is made by attaching a sheet of bamboo or metal to a board that acts as a resonator. The board is held in both hands and played with the thumbs.

Most rural areas are visited regularly by a traveling movie group that brings its own equipment and movies. There are no movie theaters outside of large towns, but a traveling group can improvise, and if a suitable whitewashed wall is not available to project the movie, a large white sheet is hung over a wall as a substitute.

On the weekends, dances are held regularly in the rural areas, with perhaps an accompanying live drum band. Smaller parties are held at home whenever a suitable occasion arises, such as the birth of a child, and a radio broadcast of music provides the impetus for dancing.

A MBANGALA FOLK TALE: CHIBINDA ILUNGA

This is a folk tale of the Mbangala people of Angola that goes back centuries to the time when the Lunda kingdom was first established by people from another kingdom—the Luba—in what is now the southeastern part of the Democratic Republic of Congo.

A young prince called Chibinda Ilunga came to the Lunda kingdom because he had fallen out with the Luba king who accused Chibinda of being afraid to take up arms in war. The truth was that the Luba king was secretly jealous of Chibinda's great skill as a hunter. The queen of the Lunda people, called Lueji, was down by the riverside one morning when she came across Chibinda for the first time. She was struck by his great beauty and natural manners and before the day had passed they had fallen in love with each other.

In time they married and in due course Lueji announced to her court that Chibinda was now their king. He made a speech to the court and promised that as a hunter he would continue to kill animals, but that he would never shed the blood of another human being. This was accepted, but a problem arose when Lueji was unable to bear children. The difficulty was solved when Lueji found another woman, called Kamonga, who also became Chibinda's wife and bore him children.

SPORTS

Sports are tremendously popular in Angola. The sports that attract the most participants and spectators are soccer, basketball, handball, swimming, and roller hockey. In 1980 Angola won the African men's junior basketball championship. In 1989, 1991, and 1993 the national basketball team were African champions. In track and field Angola has also enjoyed success. In the 1988 All-African Championships in Algeria, long-jumper António Santos won a gold medal for Angola.

Soccer is very popular, not least because it only requires a ball for 22 people to enjoy a game. Angola has a professional soccer league, but the best players are lured away to Portugal because of the higher wages players can command there. Despite this, the Angolan national team reached the finals of the 1996 African Cup. In large towns it is not unusual for 75,000 spectators to fill the stadium if one of the top clubs is playing.

Angolan women have also achieved notable success in sports. In handball, the women have won three African championships—in 1986, 1989, and 1994. All three titles were won while playing in other countries.

An Angolan athlete trains for the Olympic Games.

CHESS CHAMPIONS

A successful tradition of competing in international chess competitions began in 1987 when, at age 17, Manuel Mateus became the youngest African player to gain the international status of chess master. Today, Angola can boast of nearly a dozen chess players ranked as international masters and chess is a popular extracurricular activity in high schools.

FESTIVALS

PEOPLE IN ANGOLA ARE MORE LIKELY to remember festivals of the past than to participate in contemporary ones. In particular, traditional Angolan society celebrated important events in a person's life. The birth of a child, the coming of age from adolescence to adulthood, marriage, and death were all marked as important social occasions and, apart from death, were celebrated as festive occasions.

It is not that festivals are no longer celebrated in Angola, only that nowadays many people find it difficult to afford the food and drink that traditionally characterized a festival. The fracturing and separation of so many families because of the war has also meant that it is more difficult for family members to come together for a festive occasion. If the present peace does last, there is good reason to hope that in time the traditional exuberance that marked festive occasions will once again become a lively aspect of Angolan society.

Carnival time—Angolans party in Menongue (*opposite*) and watch celebrations in Lunda Norte (*left*).

A mother with her baby. It is an Angolan custom for the family of the father to name the first-born child in a family.

FAMILY FESTIVALS

In Angola, communities enjoy the often impromptu social festivals that take place for occasions such as the birth of a child. The birth of a child is always a cause for celebration, and even among poor families, the occasion is marked in some way. A special meal is usually cooked at the earliest opportunity, often for the evening of the day when the child is born. Even if the mother travels to a clinic for the actual birth, she is usually back home the same day.

To prepare for the celebratory meal, a chicken or a duck is often considered necessary. Sometimes a family member may make a present of one of their chickens or ducks and it will be killed and prepared within an hour. Neighbors will almost certainly pay a visit to wish the newborn a prosperous and happy future and a small amount of money will be given as a gift for the child. The home needs to be cleaned up and made as presentable as possible for the visitors. If there is money for beer a few bottles are bought and offered to guests.

The baptism of a child, a Christian ceremony marking a spiritual stage in a child's life, is often followed by a small private celebration for family and neighbors. When a child reaches its first birthday, parents and neighbors may also celebrate the occasion. When a daughter reaches the age of 18, her parents may present her to the community in a "coming out" party. In a small village this could include nearly all of the villagers, although in a town the party would be only be attended by family, friends, and neighbors.

CHRISTMAS AND EASTER

Christmas Day is usually celebrated in Angola with a special meal. Families try to gather as many members of the family as possible for the meal. They also try to save for the Christmas meal to be able afford, for example, swordfish instead of a less expensive type of fish. Christians celebrate Christmas for its religious significance because the day is traditionally regarded as the birthday of Jesus Christ. Even non-Christians are likely to regard the day as a time for general goodwill and merriment. For the average Angolan, Christmas is more of a family occasion than a religious event.

Easter, which celebrates the belief that Christ was resurrected after his crucifixion, is the most important festival for Roman Catholics. Easter Sunday, the focus of Easter, takes place between late March and late April, depending on the date of the first full moon after the spring equinox. The weeks before Easter are known as Lent and they are traditionally observed as a period of abstinence to commemorate Christ's 40-day fast in the wilderness. In Angola this tradition of abstinence is reflected in the practice of not eating meat during Lent.

With more than one billion Christians around the world, Christmas and Easter are among the world's most widely observed celebrations.

FUNERALS

A funeral, known as a *komba* ("KUM-ba") in Angola, is not always as somber an affair as it is in the West. In traditional rural areas, it is believed that the deceased will be happy if everyone celebrates. The *komba* is organized by close relatives and friends, and between them, they cover the cost of the food and drink that is served to those who attend the funeral. Often the close friends are neighbors of the deceased, as in Angolan villages neighbors can become very close and be regarded as almost part of the family.

A Herero family. The Herero make up a small minority of the population.

MARRIAGE

In the countryside, it is not uncommon for Angolan parents to suggest a possible partner for their son or daughter. In some rural areas, this goes a step further, with arranged marriages still taking place regularly. However, in urban areas this practice is in decline and it is more common for parents to simply pass on to their daughter a compliment that a man may have made. A compliment is made on the understanding that this might be interpreted as the first stage in a proposal of marriage.

However a marriage is arrived at, the event is a cause for celebration. Once the compulsory registration in a government office has taken place, there may be a church ceremony in which the bride wears white and the groom dresses up in a suit and tie. In practice, many young couples will not be able to afford a white dress or a suit. But this will not prevent a celebration. A special meal is prepared, drinks will be available, and a party atmosphere helps transform the event into a festive occasion. Singing and dancing always accompany the party.

CIRCUMCISION

The masked figure of the ndzingi is one of the most popular figures at circumcision festivals among the Mbwela people. The ndzingi first instills fear because of his frightful appearance, characterized by his large red-colored mouth, but this fear turns to laughter when he falls to the ground because his head is too large.

Young boys in the audience run up and help him upright—but to no avail because he collapses again. The combination of feelings evoked by the dance—first fear and then the relief of laughter—matches the emotions of many boys taking part in the circumcision ceremony.

A masked dancer in an initiation ceremony in Huíla province.

CARNIVAL

Carnival is the most popular celebration in Angola. It used to be celebrated at the end of March each year, marking the anniversary of the expulsion of invading South African troops. Carnival has now been moved to February. In Luanda Carnival is celebrated on the streets with processions. The most striking aspect of the festivities are the colorful and elaborately-decorated floats that make up the main procession.

A prize is awarded for the most impressive float, and various groups spend a lot of time in designing and decorating their floats in the hope that they might win the prize. Such is the popularity of Carnival in Luanda that troupes drive to the capital from rural areas in trucks, bringing their floats fully or partly made. When the main procession through the streets is over, the carnival spirit continues until late in the night.

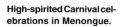

High-spirited Carnival celebrations in Menongue.

When the Portuguese government granted Angola independence on November 11, 1975, the MPLA established a government in Luanda under the presidency of the movement's leader, Agostinho Neto. UNITA and the FNLA established a rival coalition government, based in Huambo.

ANGOLAN PUBLIC HOLIDAYS

The following are some of the public holidays celebrated in Angola:

New Year's Day	January 1
Anniversary of the start of the war of independence against Portuguese colonialism	February 4
Easter	variable
May Day	May 1
National Heroes Day (Birthday of Agostinho Neto)	September 17
Independence Day	November 11
Christmas Day	December 25

FOOD

FOR THE MAJORITY OF ANGOLANS, finding food is at the heart of their struggle for survival. The idea of dining as a form of entertainment or being able to make choices about what to eat rarely finds expression for most people in Angola.

A typical poor family usually does not eat meat because it cannot afford to do so. Only for special occasions is a family-owned chicken or duck killed and cooked.

The inhabitants of Luanda and other large towns depend on imported food, but the rest of the population, living in the countryside, live off what they can grow, plus whatever small income might be available from selling surplus food.

Opposite: **Women pound cassava. The root vegetable is an important part of the Angolan diet.**

Left: **A large market on the outskirts of Luanda attracts crowds of sellers and buyers every day.**

SURVIVAL TACTICS

Corn is a crop that provides a rich source of starch as well as protein. However, the cultivation of corn requires regular weeding and a degree of care on the part of the farmer. Angolans have responded to war conditions by using land traditionally reserved for corn for the cultivation of millet, cassava, sweet potatoes, and sorghum.

Millet, for example, is also a cereal grass, but it grows more rapidly than corn and requires less weeding. Sorghum is far more resistant to drought than corn and consequently requires less watering. People have also survived by exploiting to the full any opportunity to fish in streams or

Bananas at a market in Uíge province, near the border with the Democratic Republic of Congo.

lagoons. In the past, this was regarded as a secondary activity for women, but it is now practiced by all members of the family.

In Luanda and other large towns a limited form of agriculture has developed amid the tin shacks and concrete buildings. Pigs are a familiar sight in Luanda, with children often employed to keep a watchful eye on this valuable source of food. Wherever possible, a family keeps a few chickens, or goats as well, and the care of these animals often falls to the women and children in a family.

CASSAVA

Cassava is the most important food crop in Angola. It can be made into a variety of foods—cassava flour, bread, tapioca—and even a laundry starch. An alcoholic brew can also be made from cassava. The raw root of the cassava is poisonous—it contains a cyanide-based sugar—and requires careful preparation before it is safe to be eaten.

Traditionally, the cassava root is processed by women. The first stage involves soaking the root and allowing it to dry completely in the open. It is then pounded into a flour using a mortar and pestle. Before the root is harvested the leaves of the plant can be removed and used to make *kizaka* ("kiz-AH-ka"), an Angolan dish made from vegetables. Another popular and inexpensive meal based on the cassava is *fuba* ("FOO-bar"). Untreated cassava, known as *bombom* ("BOMB-bomb"), can be bought in towns by the bucketful.

A woman sells fish in Namibe province.

117

MEALS OF THE DAY

Breakfast usually consists of bread or *funje* ("PHON-jee"), a porridge made from cassava. Coffee is a popular drink. Although good quality coffee is cultivated in Angola, most people drink instant coffee imported from abroad, as it is more readily available than the superior local coffee. Young children may be fed with milk made from imported milk powder. Poorer families drink plain water. In Luanda and many other towns water has to be collected by walking to the nearest water supply and carrying back filled containers.

Lunch is often quick and informal, especially for those who work, and may consist of bread with some cheese. The evening meal on the other hand is an occasion for most of the family to be together and is often delayed until everyone has returned home.

As few people can afford meat, vegetables and fish are more commonly eaten. In the towns, meals and hot drinks are prepared using a stove fueled with bottled gas. Many homes in urban areas do not have a separate kitchen; the stove is found in the livingroom.

Some families also have a space outside their home for a small open fire, using wood and charcoal, which saves the expense of bottled gas. Some people earn their living by collecting firewood in the countryside and then selling it in towns. A small supply of paraffin is usually kept to sprinkle over the wood to make it easier to light in the morning. In the countryside, stoves are usually fueled by charcoal or coal and the cooking often takes place outside the home in the open.

Grilled fish are easy to prepare and popular in Angola.

LIVING BY BREAD ALONE

In Luanda one seldom needs to walk far before finding a bakery, as bread forms the basis of a quick lunch for many working people. Some entrepreneurs bake bread in their own homes and sell it by the roadside or in a market.

One bag of flour makes around 500 rolls, and a baker needs to know how many fresh rolls he hopes to sell before baking a new day's supply. In smaller towns and in the countryside a popular type of bread is *pao burro* ("pow BORE-o," donkey's bread), which is inexpensively baked at home in a simple wood-burning oven.

Homeless children in Luanda eat a meal of bread.

THE COST OF FOOD

The following list offers an idea of the prices of the common types of food available to the majority of the population:

Butter (US$1.20 a tin), beans (US$0.22 a pound/US$0.50 a kg), bread (US$0.10 a loaf), cassava (US$1.50 a bucket), cooking oil (US$4.50 a gallon/US$1.20 a liter), fish (US$0.22 a pound/US$0.50 a kg), corn (US$0.04 a pound/US$0.10 a kg), meat (US$0.90 a pound/US$2 a kg), milk powder (US$2 a tin), sausages (US$2.50 a tin), sugar (US$0.27 a pound/US$0.60 a kg), water (US$0.10 a bucket)

Most Angolans live on a diet that consists of these items. A typical income earned by a woman in Luanda is about US$2.50 a day, so a large proportion of the family income goes to buy food.

Fuel is also needed to cook the food. The cheapest fuels are firewood and charcoal, and the prices of these gradually increase as it becomes necessary to travel farther away from the city center to find a suitable supply.

Many households use bottled gas as their main cooking fuel. One bottle, which lasts about two weeks for an average family, costs around US$2.20.

FERMENTED CASSAVA FLOUR AND BANKU

1 cup fermented cassava flour
2 cups banku flour (other types of flour can be used)
3 cups water, add salt to taste

Bring 2 cups of salted water to a boil. Mix the cassava and banku flour with the remaining 1 cup of salted water and stir well. Add the mixture to the boiling salted water and stir until the contents begin to boil.

Then lower the heat and continue stirring for about 15 minutes, until all the water has evaporated. The mixture can then be shaped and served with fish, stew, or soup.

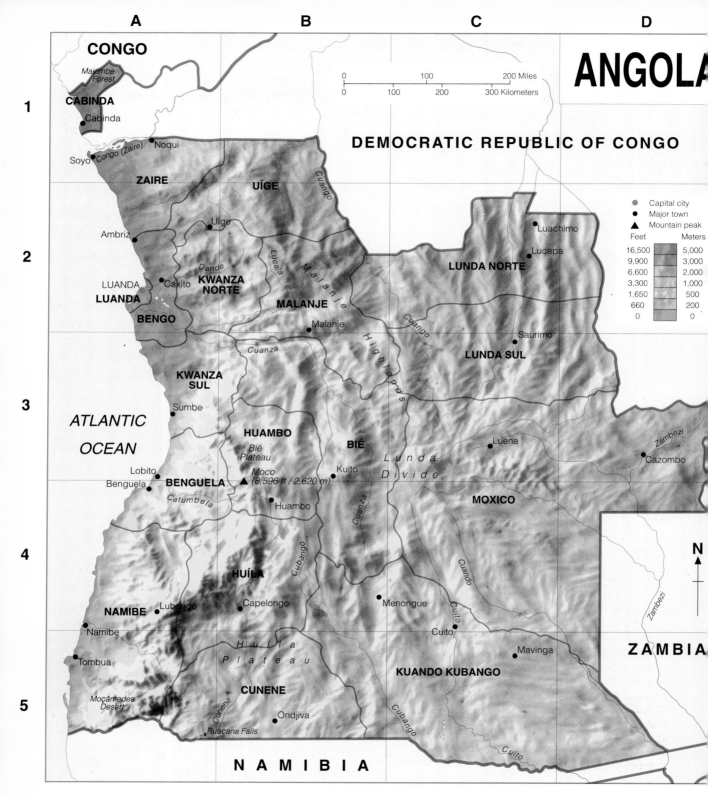

ANGOLA

CONGO

Maiombe Forest

CABINDA

Cabinda

Noqui

Soyo · Congo (Zaire)

DEMOCRATIC REPUBLIC OF CONGO

ZAIRE

UÍGE

Cuango

Uíge

Ambriz

Dande

Lucala

Malanje

Luachimo

Lucapa

LUNDA NORTE

LUANDA · Caxito

KWANZA NORTE

LUANDA

MALANJE

BENGO

Malanje

Cuango

Saurimo

LUNDA SUL

Cuanza

KWANZA SUL

Sumbe

HUAMBO

Bié Plateau

BIÉ

L u n d a

Luena

Zambezi

Cazombo

Moco
▲ *(8,596 ft / 2,620 m)*

Kuito

D i v i d e

Lobito

Benguela · **BENGUELA**

Catumbela

Huambo

Cuanza

MOXICO

Cubango

HUÍLA

Cuando

Menongue

Cuito

N

NAMIBE

Lubango

Capelongo

Cuito

ZAMBIA

Namibe

H u í l a

Mavinga

Tombua

P l a t e a u

KUANDO KUBANGO

Moçâmedes Desert

CUNENE

Cunene

Cubango

Ondjiva

Cuito

Ruacana Falls

ATLANTIC OCEAN

N A M I B I A

Capital city
Major town
Mountain peak

Feet	Meters
16,500	5,000
9,900	3,000
6,600	2,000
3,300	1,000
1,650	500
660	200
0	0

0   100   200 Miles
0   100   200   300 Kilometers

A   B   C   D

1   2   3   4   5

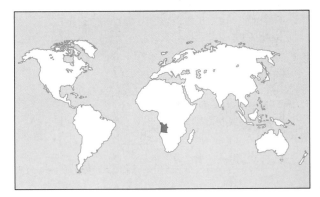

QUICK NOTES

AREA
481,354 square miles
(1,246,700 square km)

POPULATION
13 million (1998 UN estimate)

CAPITAL
Luanda

OFFICIAL NAME
The Republic of Angola

OFFICIAL LANGUAGE
Portuguese

HIGHEST POINT
Mount Moco (8,596 ft / 2,620 m)

MAIN ETHNIC GROUPS
Ovimbundu, Mbundu, Bakongo

MAIN RELIGIONS
Traditional African beliefs, Christianity

RIVERS
Cuanza, Congo, Cunene

CLIMATE
Tropical, with low rainfall in the west but increasing inland

MAJOR CITIES
Huambo, Lobito, Benguela, Lubango, Malanje, Namibe

PROVINCES
Bengo, Benguela, Bié, Cabinda, Cunene, Huambo, Huíla, Kuando Kubango, Kwanza Norte, Kwanza Sul, Luanda, Lunda Norte, Lunda Sul, Malanje, Moxico, Namibe, Uíge, Zaire

NATIONAL FLAG
Two equal horizontal stripes of red and black, with a five-pointed star, half a cog-wheel, and a machete superimposed in the center in gold

CURRENCY
The kwanza
1 kwanza = 100 lwei
US$1 = 265,000 kwanza

MAIN EXPORTS
Crude oil, diamonds, refined oil, gas

MAJOR IMPORTS
Electrical and transport equipment, animal and vegetable products, food and beverages

POLITICAL LEADERS
José Eduardo dos Santos—president since 1979
Agostinho Neto—president from 1975 to 1979

MAIN POLITICAL PARTIES
Popular Movement for the Liberation of Angola (MPLA)
National Union for the Total Independence of Angola (UNITA)

ANNIVERSARY
Independence Day (November 11)

GLOSSARY

assimilado ("ass-sim-ill-AD-o")
Special status given to Angolans who adopted the Portuguese way of life during colonial rule.

bombom ("BOMB-bomb")
Untreated cassava.

caderneta ("KAD-er-ne-ta")
Special identity cards carried by Angolans during Portuguese colonial rule.

compra e venda ("COM-pra a VEN-dar")
Buy and sell.

fetish
Term for describing an object that is worshipped by a people because of a belief in the object's magical or spiritual quality.

fuba ("FOO-bar")
Popular meal based on the cassava.

funje ("PHON-jee")
Porridge made from cassava.

gouache ("gwash")
Method of painting that uses opaque pigments ground in water and mixed with a glue-like substance.

kimbanda ("kim-BAN-da")
Diviner or witch doctor.

kizaka ("kiz-AH-ka")
Dish made from vegetables.

komba ("KUM-ba")
Funeral.

maka ("MAR-ka")
African word meaning "problem" that has entered the Portuguese spoken in Angola.

makisi avamala ("ma-KI-si a-va-MAR-la")
Masks worn by male dancers of the Mbwela tribe.

makisi avampwevo ("ma-KI-si a-vam-PWEV-o")
"Masks" worn by female dancers of the Mbwela tribe.

masemba ("MASS-m-ba")
A type of dance popular in Luanda where a pair of dancers thrust their stomachs toward one another.

musseque ("MUS-seek")
Shantytown.

pao burro ("pow BORE-o")
Bread popular in smaller towns and in the countryside.

saxi ("SAR-ki")
A type of percussion instrument.

sagaya ("sar-GA-ya")
A musical instrument of the Humbi tribe, made from an ordinary hunting bow and a mouth brace.

BIBLIOGRAPHY

Ayo, Yvonne. *Eyewitness Africa*. London: Dorling Kindersley, 1995.

Britten, Victoria. *Death of Dignity*. London: Pluto Books, 1998.

Somerville, Keith. *Angola: Politics, Economics, and Society (Marxist Regimes Series)*. Boulder, Colorado: L. Rienner Publishers, 1986.

van der Winden, Bob, ed. *A Family of the Musseque*. Oxford, England: WorldView Publishing, 1996.

Warner, Rachel. *Refugees*. Hove, England: Wayland (Publishers) Ltd, 1996.

Watson, James. *No Surrender: A Story of Angola*. London: Lions Tracks, 1992.

INDEX

INDEX

INDEX